EDGE BOOKS™

The Amazingly GROSS Human Body

The SWEATY Book of SWEAT

by Kelly Regan Barnhill

Consultant:
Michael Bentley
Professor of Biology
Minnesota State University, Mankato

Capstone press®

Mankato, Minnesota

Edge Books are published by Capstone Press,
151 Good Counsel Drive, P.O. Box 669, Mankato, Minnesota 56002.
www.capstonepress.com

Library of Congress Cataloging-in-Publication Data
Barnhill, Kelly Regan.
   The sweaty book of sweat / By Kelly Regan Barnhill.
   p. cm. — (Edge books. The amazingly gross human body)
   Includes bibliographical references and index.
   Summary: "Describes the gross qualities of sweat, and how it works to
benefit a person's health" — Provided by publisher.
   ISBN 978-1-4296-3353-6 (library binding)
   1. Perspiration — Juvenile literature. I. Title. II. Series.
QP221.B37 2010
612.7'921 — dc22   2009005507

Editorial Credits
Aaron Sautter, editor; Kyle Grenz, designer; Jo Miller, media researcher

Photo Credits
BigStockPhoto.com/silverbelle1, 15
Capstone Press/Karon Dubke, cover (all), 5, 7, 8, 11, 12, 13, 14, 19, 22, 24, 25,
      26 (girl), 27, 28
CDC/Janice Haney Car, 26 (inset)
Getty Images Inc./Brian Bahr, 16
iStockphoto/Jim Kolaczko, 4; Nathan Gleave, 21
Shutterstock/Filipe B. Varela, borders; Sebastian Kaulitzki, 10; Shane White, 20
Superstock, Inc., 29

TABLE of CONTENTS

HOT and SWEATY

It's 3:00 in the afternoon, and the soccer game is in its second overtime. The hot afternoon sun beats down on everyone. Fans swig cold water between cheers. There's no shade, no breeze, and no relief from the heat.

The soccer players race by, kicking the ball with all their might. Sweat beads up on their foreheads, arms, and legs. Drops of sweat trickle down their backs. Their hair and shirts are soaked.

GROSS FACT

On average, adults produce more than 2 quarts (1.9 liters) of sweat each day.

HEALTHY SWEATING

Everybody sweats. We sweat when we exercise. We sweat when we're hot. We sweat when we're nervous or scared. We sweat all the time. Sweat usually dries so fast that we don't even know it's there. But when we get hot, it pools under our arms, runs down our necks, and soaks our hair. Sometimes it stings our eyes and drips off our noses. Worst of all, it makes us stink.

Sweat can be pretty annoying sometimes. But life would be very different for us if we didn't sweat. Slimy, stinky sweat is one of the many gross things our bodies use to stay healthy. Nobody wants to get too close to a bunch of sweaty soccer players, but we should still be happy to sweat. Let's take a look at the reasons why.

the WET STUFF

When you get too warm, sweat drips off your skin and soaks through your clothes. Have you ever wondered what's in that wet stuff? Why do we sweat anyway?

WHAT'S IN SWEAT?

Sweat, or perspiration, is made by millions of tiny glands in our skin. Sweat is mostly water. But it has tiny amounts of **urea** and salt mixed in too. These chemicals are the reason why sweat tastes salty and stings your eyes.

urea a waste product made by your body's cells; most urea is removed from your body by your kidneys.

skin surface

hair follicle

sweat glands

fat cells

As you eat, work, and play, your body's cells are constantly producing the energy you need. As the cells use the nutrients from the food you eat, they produce urea and other **toxins**. These waste products can become dangerous if they build up in your body. Most of them are filtered out by your **kidneys** and come out in your pee. But small amounts of them come out in your sweat too.

GROSS FACT

Most adults have an average of 2.6 million sweat glands in their skin.

toxin   a poisonous substance made by your body's cells

kidney   an organ that filters blood and makes pee

TYPES OF SWEAT

You have two kinds of sweat glands. Each kind makes a different type of sweat. Eccrine glands produce most of the sweat on your body. These glands cover your head, face, arms, back, and legs. The sweat made by eccrine glands is thin and clear. It's mostly water with some salt and urea mixed in.

Sweat glands on your head and face produce clear sweat.

12

Sweat glands in your armpits produce thicker, yellowish sweat.

Appocrine glands are found in your armpits and groin area. They are also in the palms of your hands and the soles of your feet. Appocrine glands produce thicker, light yellow sweat that can stain the armpits of a white T-shirt. This sweat looks different because it contains fatty acids in addition to salt and urea.

KEEPING YOU COOL

Sweat has some gross ingredients, but it has an important job to do. Sweat is part of the body's system for cooling itself. When you sweat, the heat from your skin helps the sweat **evaporate**. This process results in less heat on your skin, so you feel cooler.

evaporate — to change from a liquid into a gas

Evaporation works best when there is some wind to dry your sweat.

HOW DO PETS STAY COOL?

Dogs and cats can't sweat like humans to stay cool. You've probably seen dogs panting on a hot summer day. Dogs have many blood vessels in their mouths and tongues. Panting causes their saliva to evaporate, which cools the blood flowing through their mouths. The cooled blood then helps to keep a dog's whole body cool.

Your pet's fur doesn't just keep it warm in cold weather, either. Believe it or not, it also protects your pet from the heat. The long hair acts as a barrier between the warm air and your pet's skin.

USEFUL SWEAT

Athletes sweat a lot to stay cool, even when it's cold outside.

Just like a car's engine, your body needs fuel, water, and oxygen to work correctly. Also like a car engine, your body needs to stay cool. If you get too hot, your body's organs could begin shutting down, and you might die.

THE BODY'S THERMOSTAT

When your muscles work hard, they generate heat. Have you ever noticed that you get warm while playing outside on a cold day? Your skin is keeping your body heat from escaping. Of course, it's not a perfect system. You still need to wear a warm coat on cold winter days.

But when your body gets too hot, another system is needed to help you cool off. Cars have a temperature gage that warns people when the engine overheats. People also have a temperature gage. It tells your body when it's time to start making more sweat.

SENDING SIGNALS

Your skin is covered with tiny nerve endings. These nerve endings are very sensitive. They can sense how warm or cool you are. When your brain gets the signal that you're too warm, it tells your sweat glands that it's time to cool things off. Sweat then begins oozing out to help cool down your skin.

Your body also sends more blood to your skin. This is why your skin might turn red in hot weather or during exercise. The blood running through blood vessels under your skin is cooled by the evaporating sweat. The cooled blood then cycles through your body to reduce your body temperature. Your body's internal thermostat keeps the temperature just right so your body's organs continue working correctly.

People's faces often turn red when they get too warm.

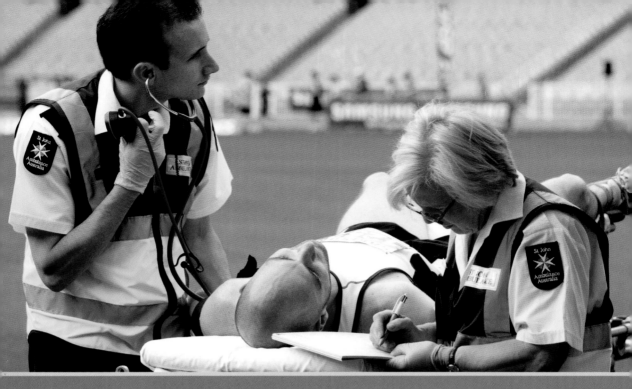

People suffering from heat stroke can die if they aren't treated right away.

HEAT STROKE

Sweat is great at keeping us cool. But sometimes, even buckets of sweat can't cool down the body fast enough. Heat stroke is a serious medical condition that happens when the body gets too hot. It can cause you to feel sick or dizzy, or even faint. In the worst cases, it causes seizures, organ failure, and death. Heat stroke often happens on humid summer days. When there is a lot of moisture in the air, it's harder for a person's sweat to evaporate.

People should watch for a major warning sign of heat stroke. If you stop sweating, it's time to cool off fast. When people stop sweating, it means they are dehydrated. Their bodies don't have enough water to keep working properly. If you're playing outside and you notice that your skin is hot and dry, it's time to stop. Find some shade and drink some cold water. Heat stroke isn't just uncomfortable — it can be deadly.

UGH! What's That SMELL?

You may be surprised to learn that sweat doesn't have an odor. So how do sweaty people get so stinky? To answer that question, you need to know a little more about your body. Brace yourself — it's not pretty.

HITCHING A RIDE

Take a good look at your skin. You might see a few freckles and some fine hairs. There may also be a little dirt or some leftover sunscreen. But there's something else there you can't see — lots of bacteria and other **microbes**. Entire colonies of microbes live on your skin all the time. They don't wash off, and you can't rub them off either. In fact, it's impossible to get rid of them. And you wouldn't want to.

microbe — a tiny living thing that you can't see without a microscope

OUR GERMY FRIENDS

The bacteria that live on your skin are actually good germs that serve a very important purpose. They make it harder for harmful germs to live on your skin and cause an **infection**. If good germs already cover your body, there's no place for the bad ones to live, eat, and grow.

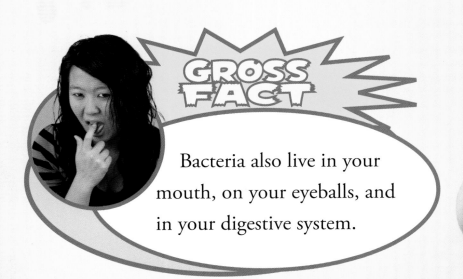

GROSS FACT

Bacteria also live in your mouth, on your eyeballs, and in your digestive system.

infection – an illness caused by germs

You can't see bacteria, but your skin is
covered with millions of them.

Sweat smells bad because of the waste products left behind by bacteria on your skin.

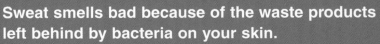

OUR SMELLY NEIGHBORS

So the bacteria on your skin are good — most of the time. But there's one problem. Sweat is full of stuff that bacteria love to snack on. When bacteria eat, they multiply — a lot. And they leave behind waste products. After awhile, all that waste created by millions of bacteria starts to stink. It isn't really your sweat that people smell. It's the bacteria's waste floating in your sweat that stinks!

GROSS FACT

Sometimes sweat smells because of the foods we eat. If you eat foods with a lot of garlic, your sweat might also smell like garlic.

GROSS, YET AMAZING SWEAT

A sweaty body often means a stinky body. And those yellow stains on your shirts aren't pretty. But without sweat, life would be very unpleasant. The next time you're soaked with sweat on a hot day, remember that it's really a good thing. Sweating is just one of the many gross — but amazing — ways your body helps keep you healthy.

EGYPTIAN CLEANLINESS

It's not just modern people who think sweat smells bad. The ancient Egyptians also liked to remain stink-free. But they didn't have deodorants and other products we use today. How did they keep from smelling sour in the heat?

The first thing they did was remove body hair. Women usually shaved under their arms. Men shaved their faces, armpits, chests, and even their heads. Shaving allowed air to flow better around the body to help stay cool. The Egyptians also bathed often to remove dirt, grime, and sweat. They used a lot of perfume too. Ancient Egypt was once the biggest producer of perfumes in the world.

GLOSSARY

bacteria (bak-TEER-ee-uh) — one-celled, microscopic living things that exist all around you and inside you; many bacteria are useful, but some cause disease.

evaporate (i-VA-puh-rayt) — to change from a liquid into a vapor or a gas

gland (GLAND) — an organ that produces chemicals or substances that are used by the body

infection (in-FEK-shuhn) — an illness caused by germs

kidney (KID-nee) — an organ that filters waste products from the blood and turns them into urine

microbe (MYE-krobe) — a tiny living thing that is too small to be seen without a microscope

nutrient (NOO-tree-uhnt) — a substance needed by a living thing to stay healthy; vitamins are nutrients.

seizure (SEE-zhur) — a sudden attack of illness, or a spasm

toxin (TOK-sin) — a poisonous substance produced inside the body as waste

urea (yoo-REE-uh) — a waste product produced by the body's cells; most urea is removed by your kidneys.

READ MORE

Lew, Kristi. *Itch and Ooze: Gross Stuff On Your Skin.* Gross Body Science. Minneapolis: Millbrook Press, 2010.

Parker, Steve. *Human Body: An Interactive Guide to the Inner Workings of the Body.* Discoverology. Hauppauge, New York: Barrons Educational Series, 2008.

Walker, Richard. *Dr. Frankenstein's Human Body Book: The Monstrous Truth About How Your Body Works.* New York: DK, 2008.

INTERNET SITES

FactHound offers a safe, fun way to find Internet sites related to this book. All of the sites on FactHound have been researched by our staff.

Here's all you do:

Visit *www.facthound.com*

FactHound will fetch the best sites for you!

INDEX